Columba

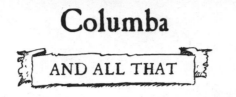

AND ALL THAT

Columba

AND ALL THAT

Allan Burnett

Illustrated by Scoular Anderson

BIRLINN

First published in 2007 by
Birlinn Limited
West Newington House
10 Newington Road
Edinburgh
EH9 1QS

www.birlinn.co.uk

ISBN13: 978 1 84158 571 0
ISBN10: 1 84158 571 8

British Library Cataloguing-in-Publication Data
A catalogue record for this book is available from the British Library

Designed by James Hutcheson
Typeset by Iolaire Typesetting, Newtonmore
Printed and bound by Cox & Wyman Ltd, Reading

For Roan

Contents

The monster lay still and silent on the riverbed. High above, it could see human arms and legs furiously pounding the surface. Someone was trying to swim from one side of the River Ness to the other – and they were making the monster hungry.

The giant creature uncoiled its long, scaly tail and gave it a stretch. Then, with one muscular push, it launched itself from the riverbed towards its victim above. Breaking the surface of the river, it let out a deafening roar.

The swimmer, a young man in a tunic, jerked up his head. He could see the monster coming right at him. He tried to swim away but his muscles were suddenly weak with terror.

The huge creature rose up from the water and opened its giant, gaping jaws. It was going to bite off the young man's head. One gulp would do it. The youngster shut his eyes. There was a blood-curdling scream . . .

A voice bellowed from the shore. The giant fish froze.

'DO NOT TOUCH HIM!'

Slowly, the monster pulled back. The boy still didn't open his eyes.

Now it was the beast's turn to tremble with fear. With its mouth still hanging open, it looked up at the owner of the voice and saw a tall, hooded figure in a long cloak. The man raised his hand over the river and made the sign of a cross in the air. Then he fixed the quivering creature with his eyes. 'GO BACK AT ONCE,' he commanded.

The monster felt as if an unseen power had gripped him. The force pushed him back through the water, slowly at first, then faster, and faster, until suddenly it plunged him deep below the surface.

Meanwhile, still trembling with shock, the boy opened his eyes. 'It's OK,' the man on the shore reassured him. 'You'll be safe now.' Very gingerly, the boy carried on swimming across the river.

Down below, the monster thought to itself.

Back on the shore of the river, the tall man watched as the boy emerged safely on the opposite bank and waved. Standing behind the man was a group of people. None of them could believe what they had just witnessed.

'It must be magic,' someone said. 'No, it's not magic,' said someone else. 'It's a miracle.'

'He must be a wizard,' said one. 'No,' said another. 'He's much more powerful than that.'

'Who is he?' several people asked at once.

The man turned and faced them all.

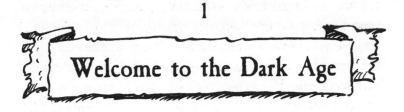

Welcome to the Dark Age

Columba was no ordinary human being. The dramatic traditional tale you have just read makes that very clear.

He was a holy man, a saint, who lived almost one and a half thousand years ago. He was very special, and his followers built a symbol so that people would remember him. Columba's symbol is a stone cross that looks like this:

It's called a Celtic cross. The circular bit is designed to hold up the heavy stone arms of the cross so that they don't fall off. If you look around today you will see thousands of these crosses – especially in Scotland and Ireland, which are the two countries where Columba's adventures happened.

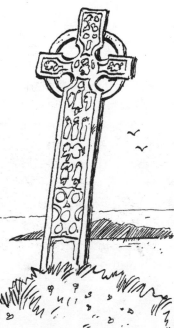

But before we find out about these adventures, we need to get something straight – the facts of his life are a bit of a mess.

How so? Well, imagine going to a Scottish or Irish churchyard. There, you see a Celtic cross that has fallen over and smashed into pieces. It's all jumbled up and a few bits are missing.

A stonemason might be able to rebuild the cross, but he or she would have to use some completely new bits. While they are at it, they might add a few elaborate decorations to make the cross more interesting.

The facts of Columba's life story are like a ruined Celtic cross. Some bits are broken, which means they don't make much sense. Some bits are missing, because people forgot how that part of the story went.

Other bits are completely new, like a repaired cross, because people have made up imaginary things to add to the story. In places, they even decorated the story by adding all sorts of extraordinary, out-of-this-world details.

6

The trouble is that it can be difficult to tell which bits of Columba's story are original and which bits were made up later. In other words, it can be tricky separating the facts from the myths and legends.

Most of what we know about Columba's life comes from a book written about him many hundreds of years ago by a man called Adomnan. Adomnan was a big fan of Columba, so he wanted to make him look good. His book is full of legendary stories about Columba, which are probably half true and half made-up or imaginary.

The episode you have just read, about Columba and the Loch Ness Monster, is a good example. When Columba made the monster swim away, that could have been a real miracle. But how much of the story is true and how much of it is made up, or mythical? That rather depends on whether or not you believe in miracles.

In Columba's day, just about everybody *did* believe in miracles. These days, we tend to take stories about miracles with a pinch of salt. In fact, historians think that many stories about Columba's life might not be true, whether miracles are involved or not. We just don't have many hard facts to go on.

That's why historians call the time when Columba was alive the 'Dark Age'. It doesn't mean that the world was a darker place – or that there was a problem with the sun. And no, it's not because electric lightbulbs hadn't been invented yet.

The Dark Age is just an old-fashioned way of saying that it's a time in history we don't know much about.

Luckily, Columba is one of the few Dark Age people that we do know something about. His life is full of excitement, adventure and extraordinary events. So let's start at the beginning . . .

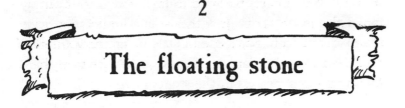

2

The floating stone

Just before Columba was born, it is said that his mum met a handsome young man who gave her some important instructions.

Columba's mum realised her baby must be special – so she followed the instructions. Sure enough, her family found the stone floating in the loch. They carried it to the place they'd been told, and little Columba was delivered there the next day. As soon as he was born, a cross-shaped niche appeared in the stone for him to lie in.

Everyone was amazed. They were even more amazed when it turned out that years ago two of Ireland's holiest people, St Brigid and St Patrick, had apparently predicted that Columba would be born.

The story of the special stone is one of many traditional tales about how Columba was born. It is a miracle story, which means it is true – but only if you believe in miracles.

But there are some things that everyone is pretty sure about – starting with where Columba was born. Columba came from Ireland, the huge island that lies across the sea to the west of Scotland, Wales and England. He probably was born in a part of Ireland called Donegal. It is thought that he came from a village called Gartan.

His birthday is said to have been on a Thursday in the year 521. Some say the date of his birth was 7 December.

So, leaving miracles aside, we know the place, day and the date of Columba's birth. Who said learning the facts of his life was difficult?

There's only one slight problem – 7 December didn't fall on a Thursday in 521. Hmmm. One of those facts must be wrong!

Unfortunately we don't have a birth certificate to solve this problem, because there was no such thing in Columba's day. But there is an explanation that might help. It seems people might have become confused about which day Columba was born on because they believed that he was able to protect people from thunder and lightning.

What does that have to do with his birthday? Well, Thursday is named after a Viking god called Thor. It mean's 'Thor's day'. And Thor was the God of Thunder. See the connection?

Viking gods like Thor were not known about in Scotland until a couple of hundred years after Columba died, but don't worry – there is an explanation for that, too. Thor is simply the Viking name for an older god called Jupiter. So when Columba was around, Thursday was known as – you guessed it – Jupiter's day.

Jupiter and Thor are not the only brain-teasing names in Columba's story. Take Columba's dad, for example. He was called Fedelmid mac Ferguso. Now that's a fancy name, but his mum's was simpler. She was called Eithne.

Mind you Eithne's dad, Columba's granddad, had a pretty far-out name. He was called Mac Naue. It means 'son of a ship'. Was he given birth to by a ship, like an alien appearing from the door of a spacecraft? That's very unlikely indeed! Perhaps his mum gave birth to him on an ordinary ship at sea.

Columba's other granddad – his dad's dad – was from an important family. They had a legendary ancestor called Conall. So the whole clan called themselves 'Children of Conall'. Or, in Irish Gaelic, the Cenel Conaill.

The Children of Conall had another ancestor, called Niall Noigiallach, who was Conall's father. Niall Noigiallach was also the high king of Ireland. His name had a scary meaning – 'Neil of the Nine Hostages'. Apparently, he took one hostage from each of the important tribes across Ireland. The tribes had to be loyal to him, or else!

So Columba was born into one of Ireland's royal families. Right from the word go, whether or not Columba was born on a special stone, he was no ordinary Joe.

Even his name was unusual – in fact, it wasn't even a regular name at all, but a nickname. So how did he get it?

Columba's Family Tree

NIALL NOIGIALLACH

Columba's grandad CONALL

Columba's other grandad MACNAUE

Columba's dad FEDELMID MACFERGUSO

Columba's mum EITHNE

COLUMBA

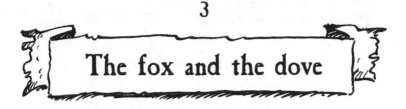

3

The fox and the dove

The first name Columba's parents chose for him wasn't Columba at all. It was Crimthann – which is a bit of a mouthful. This name means the 'Fox' or the 'Sneaky One'. Maybe his mum and dad thought he would grow up to be a naughty wee boy?

On the other hand the kids who played with him, including his wee brother and three sisters, seem to have thought he was peaceful and friendly – like a dove. So they decided to call him 'Colum Cille'.

Colum Cille means 'Dove of the Church'. So maybe his friends thought more highly of him than his parents!

Colum Cille is an Irish Gaelic name. Irish Gaelic was what the kids in Donegal spoke when they played together.

But at school, some lucky Irish children also learned to speak, read and write Latin. This was a language used for worshipping God and other important business. And the Latin for Colum Cille was . . . guess what?

A	Columbiad
B	Columbus
C	Columba
D	Columbo

Was it 'A'? Well that was actually a cannon. The columbiad was used to blast soldiers to smithereens during the American War of Independence.

Now, 'B' is an interesting one. Columbus was a sailor who left Spain and crossed the Atlantic to discover America in 1492. Mind you, the Native Americans and even the Vikings were there before him, but that's another story . . .

So what about 'C' and 'D'? Well Columbo is an American TV detective from the 1970s. He wore a crumpled raincoat and always acted the fool – but really he was very smart.

In fact, Columbo was so smart that he would have had no problem figuring out that the answer was, of course, 'C' – Columba!

Funnily enough, there are some historians who believe we don't *really* know what Columba's true name was at all. They reckon the name 'Columba' was made up by other people long after he died.

For now, let's just say that the reports you have heard about how he got his name are correct and Columba's real name was, er . . . Columba.

Now we've got all that cleared up, what did Columba want to be when he grew up? Well, you have already had some clues:

1 He was a holy man.

2 He said his birth was predicted by Saint Patrick and Saint Brigid.

3 His name means Dove of the Church.

ANSWER - You've guessed it - he joined the church and trained as a PRIEST. It's said he was sent to a foster father - Cruithnechan - who was a priest and trained Columba in the ways of God and the Christian Church.

The Christian Church in those days was powerful. What's more, people believed that churchmen had special powers. Churchmen, such as priests, were the heroes of their day. They were like politicians – except more honest. Or rock stars – but better behaved. Or magicians – only more powerful.

Even though the Christian Church was strong, it was still quite new. The Christian religion only became well known in Ireland about a hundred and fifty years before Columba was born. Before that, people didn't believe in God. They worshipped lots of different gods and they believed in magic. In fact, many people still believed in magic in Columba's day.

So when Cruithnechan taught Columba how to practise the Christian religion, it was a bit like a sorcerer teaching his apprentice how to use magic. Except, like other Christians, Cruithnechan and Columba believed their special powers were given to them by God.

Thanks to his foster-father, our hero apparently became a very successful priest when he grew up. Some reports say that the first sign of his success was that he built a monastery in Ireland.

A monastery is a place where churchmen called monks pray and hang out together. It is not to be confused with a zoo, which is where mon*keys* play and hang out together.

Unlike monkeys, monks did a lot of work in their monasteries. A monastery was like a school or university – it was a place where you could learn about all sorts of important stuff, especially God and religion.

Also unlike monkeys, monks cut their hair. In fact they cut it into a strange shape called a 'tonsure'. Celtic monks like Columba cut their tonsures so that the front of their head was completely bald and the back was long and flowing. So a monastery was a bit like a hair salon, too, where you perhaps read such magazines as *Monk's Monthly* or *Gossip Gospel* while you waited.

After building his first monastery, Columba might have built a few more – like a hairdresser building a chain of salons. Building – or 'founding', which is another word for building – monasteries gave Columba another title. He became known as an abbot, which means the leader of a monastery.

Being an abbot kept Columba busy, but it could be a very difficult job . . .

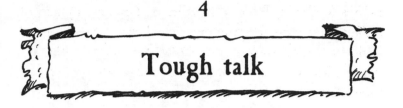

4

Tough talk

One day, when Columba was visiting one of his new monasteries, a crowd gathered around him. In the crowd there was a boy known to be very naughty. The rest of the villagers looked down on him because of his bad behaviour.

As Columba walked through the crowd, the boy tried to sneak up behind him without Columba noticing. But with his special powers, it seems that Columba could see what was going on. He reached around and gently grabbed the boy by the neck, then brought the youngster round to face him.

21

Columba told the boy to stick out his tongue. Then he reached forward and blessed it with a sign of the cross.

From now on, don't be hard on this boy. Give him a chance and he will grow up to be a fine young man - a great credit to your village.

This was a prophecy – a prediction about the future that people believed was certain to come true, because of Columba's special powers.

The villagers did as they were told and, years later, the boy apparently grew up to be a great man who became famous throughout Ireland.

That doesn't mean Columba was nice to people all the time. He believed that everyone who did something wrong deserved a second chance to change their ways – but some bad men are just plain bad! In fact, when grown-ups got on the wrong side of Columba he could be harsh.

One such grown-up was called Neman. He did all kinds of bad things – probably stealing and beating up innocent people. He had made a lot of enemies. A traditional tale tells us that, one day, Columba visited him to try to change his ways. But Neman just laughed in Columba's face.

Have it your way! But be warned – one day your enemies will turn up when you are lying in bed and slaughter you!

Oh, go away with your silly prophecies and special powers!

Years later, when Neman was lying in bed, we are told that his enemies turned up just as Columba predicted. They hadn't come to tuck Neman in, or read him a bedtime story. They pulled out their swords and cut off his head!

Whether or not Columba really could see the future, it seems that few people who crossed him lived to tell the tale. On another occasion, Columba went to visit a rich man who was known to be very mean. Columba hoped he could persuade the man to be kinder. But when Columba turned up at his house, the rich man ignored Columba and refused to meet him.

Columba wasn't impressed. He predicted that the rich man would lose all his money and then die a horrible death. Guess what? That's exactly what happened.

It's clear that Columba could be very unforgiving when he wanted to be. Even though he had God on his side, there might have been times when God did not approve of Columba's behaviour.

We can't all be perfect!

In fact, Columba might have been involved in a terrible incident that seems to have had dreadful consequences – and made God very angry with him. It might even be the reason why Columba was forced to leave Ireland in the year 563, when he was about forty-two years old, and set sail for a mysterious country called Scotland . . .

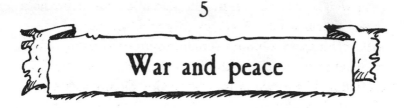

5

War and peace

Nobody knows for sure why Columba decided to leave his home in Ireland and visit Scotland. Some historians think Columba just fancied spreading his wings – like a dove – and seeing more of the world.

These historians say that Columba wanted to spread peace, love and happiness wherever he went. They think that because he was such a nice chap, he wanted to build a monastery for the people of Scotland while he was visiting. Doing so would also please God and make the Scots better people. This made Columba's trip to Scotland a special religious journey, known as a pilgrimage.

But others say that's not the real reason why Columba left Ireland. They reckon that his decision to visit Scotland wasn't made because of peace, love and happiness. In fact, they say that something very sinister forced Columba to go away in 563. So what was it?

Well, a couple of years earlier, a big, bloody battle took place in Ireland. It was called the Battle of Cul Drebene. According to some reports, Columba was involved – and he had blood on his hands.

The battle was fought between Columba's clan and another clan who lived nearby. According to reports,

Columba's enemies had wizards on their side. These wizards conjured up a mist to try to confuse their opponents.

But Columba fought back by saying a prayer and using his special powers to make the mist disappear. Now the men on his side could see their enemies clearly – and began splattering them.

Some reports say that Columba himself took out a sword and started laying in to the other side. There were even some claims that it was Columba who started the battle in the first place!

Whether Columba started the fight or not, some reports say that he was punished for taking part in the Battle of Cul Drebene. After all, hacking folks' heads off with a sword is not the sort of thing a priest – of all people – should be involved in.

The religious authorities took a while to decide on a punishment for Columba. Eventually, they decided that he should be excommunicated. Ex-comm-whatty? This is an important word, so it's worth learning. Try it slowly, like this: ex . . . comm . . . uni . . . cated. And now all together: excommunicated. Easy.

It was very nasty indeed. That's why Columba had to go to Scotland – to make up for killing people in the battle and get his punishment lifted. Scotland wasn't exactly Hell – but it was still a big scary place that he didn't know much about.

And to prove just how sorry he was, Columba had a task to perform. He had to set up a new monastery in Scotland that would help the Christian Church grow and become more powerful. Saying sorry by carrying out a task like this was known as doing a 'penance'.

There was just one problem – he had to find Scotland first. Between Ireland and Scotland lay a big, deep, roaring sea. It had been crossed before, but many of those who set sail upon it were never heard from again.

The sea was pounded by fierce gales and the boat Columba had to sail in was a tiny vessel called a currach. It was made by stretching animal skins over a wooden frame.

At least he wasn't alone. He was accompanied on the voyage by his followers, who would help him set up his monastery when they got to Scotland. According to reports, there were twelve men with Columba in the boat – the same as the number of apostles, or followers, that Jesus had. No doubt Columba was inspired by Jesus to take this number of followers with him. They included his Uncle Ernan and two cousins.

As Columba and his crew launched their craft from the shore of the north of Ireland, some reports say that seagulls chased after them. While the men rowed as hard as they could on the rising and falling waves, the birds screamed and screeched as though they were shouting 'Go back! Go back!'

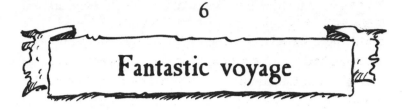

6

Fantastic voyage

These days it is easy to travel by ferry from Ireland to Scotland, but for Columba and his chums it must have been a nightmare. Even today, the sea can still be treacherous. Modern fishing boats with powerful engines are sometimes sunk by severe storms in the stretch of water between the bit of Ireland known as Ulster and the Scottish islands known as the Inner Hebrides. This was the route that Columba took in his tiny boat.

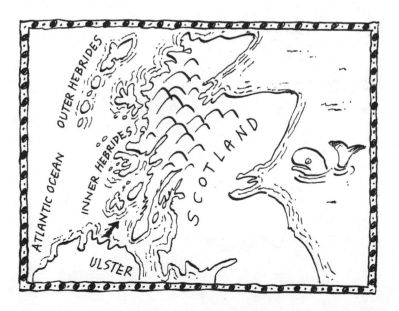

When the boat was far out at sea things got scary. The story goes that the wind dropped, or perhaps even started going in the wrong direction. This meant that Columba and his crew could have ended up miles off course. Or they might even have been lost at sea for ever. So Columba had to use his special powers. He called up a mighty wind that propelled his craft safely towards its destination.

Eventually, Columba and his friends reached an island. Today, this island is known as Oronsay. There was probably had a different name for the island back then but it seems to have been long forgotten. It *was* fifteen centuries ago, remember! Oronsay is right next to a big island known today as Colonsay.

The next island Columba and his fellow pilgrims arrived at was a different story. When he got there, apparently one of the first things he did was climb a hill and look for Ireland. He couldn't see it. So he built a cairn, which means a neat pile of stones. He built it to celebrate the fact that he had now made a completely fresh start.

He had found the island of Iona – and decided to make it his new home. But before building work began on a monastery, he must have wanted to explore the island thoroughly. So what did he find there? Was the island already inhabited by people?

Columba and his crew discovered that Iona was a very rocky island with some boggy bits and some sandy bits. It was 3 miles, or 5 kilometres, long. At its widest point it was one and a half miles, or about two and a half kilometres, across.

On the west side of Iona was the wide, roaring Atlantic Ocean. Next stop, America. Mind you, in Columba's day nobody knew America even existed!

The west side was the sandy bit of the island. The land here is known today as 'machair'. It's a good place to grow crops – which is exactly what Columba and his followers decided to do. But first they had to finish exploring the island.

After looking around for a bit, Columba and his gang – let's call them the Columbans – might have stumbled upon some mysterious ruins. These were the homes of people who had lived there many years before, during the pre-historic age. These mysterious people were 'prehistoric' because they lived before history began, which means we really know nothing about them. Columba probably didn't know much about them, either.

As for living residents, Columba might have discovered a few families living in huts dotted around the island, but we don't know for sure. It's possible that the whole place was deserted.

Once he was satisfied he had found a good spot, Columba set to work building his new monastery. The site he chose was on the east side of Iona, near to a big neighbouring island called Mull.

So what did the monastery look like?

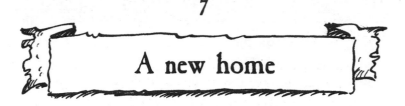

7

A new home

Columba's new monastery was mostly made of wood. It included a hut where the Columbans slept and ate their meals. Most of the Columbans slept on straw, but not Columba. According to one report, his bed was made of bare rock and his pillow was a stone. Ouch – that doesn't sound too comfortable. But as abbot of his new monastery, Columba believed he should do without creature comforts.

This was a way of showing his devotion to God – and maybe doing his penance. Remember, some historians think he might have left Ireland because he had been a bad man. Sleeping on bare stone must have given him a lot of aches and pains! Still, it showed that from now on he was trying to be a good man.

Something else Columba did to please God was fasting. This has nothing to do with doing things fast or quickly. Fasting means going without food for many days and nights, just like Jesus did in the Bible. No bread, no meat, no fish and definitely no chocolate biscuits – not that Columba had any of those, anyway.

Fasting was a way of concentrating all your thoughts on God and nothing else. When he fasted, Columba even had visions that told him secrets that nobody else knew – like what would happen in the future. But fasting was very dangerous and could only be done after a lot of careful training and preparation.

ONE DAY, WHEN COLUMBA WAS FASTING ALONE, HE HAD A TERRIBLE VISION. AN ARMY OF DEVILS ARMED WITH IRON SPIKES WAS ADVANCING TO SPLATTER ALL THE MONKS.

Oh, God! Help me!

Although Columba believed his visions were real, in truth they were probably caused by his extreme hunger. It made him dizzy and he saw and imagined things that weren't really there.

Luckily, Columba didn't have to fast and watch scary visions all the time. Back at the monastery, he was allowed to eat as usual. So thank goodness the monastery had a good kitchen.

Besides being good cooks, Columba's monks are said to have been very good at gardening. So the monastery must have had its own garden, in which vegetables were grown, as well as herbs for making medicine.

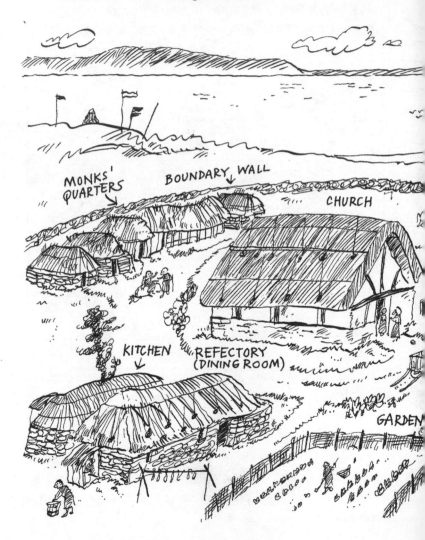

The monastery also had storehouses and a barn for animals. The monks used cows for milk, which meant they could make all sorts of mouthwatering dishes. But even milking a cow required special skills in Columba's day.

HOSTEL FOR GUESTS

MEETING ROOM

WRITING ROOM AND LIBRARY

FARM AND WORKSHOPS

THE HORRIFIED COLMAN KNEELED BEFORE COLUMBA IN SHAME.

Do not worry! Stand up, Colman. There was a devil hiding in that pail. Before pouring in the milk, you should have driven away the devil by making a sign of the cross. Bring the pail here and I will bless it now.

ONCE COLUMBA HAD DONE THIS, COLMAN'S EYES GREW AS LARGE AS SAUCERS. THE FEW DROPS OF MILK LEFT IN THE PAIL ROSE UP TO THE BRIM. THE PAIL WAS FULL AGAIN!

Now, was there really a devil in the milk pail? And did Columba really fill the milk back up again like that? Possibly not. But Columba and Colman both believed in the devil. And they believed in miracles. So maybe Columba did have the power to make the milk reappear, just like a modern magician might do today.

This doesn't mean Columba was a fraud, or a conjurer of cheap tricks. To us today, such things might seem like no more than an illusion. But if Columba and the people around him really *believed* that his powers were a gift from God, just as many religious people believe in miracles today, then it is important to respect their belief – even if you don't believe it yourself. If you can do that, you are well on the way to becoming an excellent historian.

In between marvelling at Columba's special powers, the monks got on with building more huts to extend Columba's monastery. These included a church hut, where the monks celebrated mass – which was their religious service.

Then there was another hut, where Columba and his fellow monks could write letters and poetry, compose music, sing religious songs called psalms and entertain guests. They also kept lots of books and wrote some of their own. This was the beginning of Iona's library, which grew and grew as the years passed.

But this was no ordinary library. It was a very special place . . .

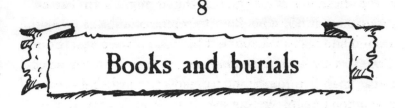

8

Books and burials

To write books in Columba's day, you needed the patience of a saint. The monastery library had to be stocked with many copies of each book, but the copying all had to be done by hand. Every single word. There were no type-writers, computers or printers in those days.

Books were written in Latin, which people from many different countries could understand – a bit like English today. Some books contained a few Gaelic words as well.

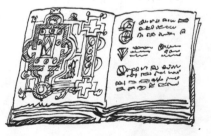

Did you know that the earliest written book with Gaelic bits might in fact have been written by Columba? It is called the *Cathach*, and it is a copy of the psalms from the Bible. Today, the *Cathach* is kept in a building called the Royal Irish Academy in Dublin.

According to some reports, books written by Columba had special powers. Once a young monk was carrying a satchel that had a book written by Columba in it. As the lad made his way across a bridge, he slipped and fell into the river. When he climbed out of the water, the satchel was soaked through and ruined. But inside the satchel Columba's book was found to be bone dry – as though it had never left the bookshelf!

A miracle? A tall tale? Or could it be that maybe, just maybe, there is a rational scientific explanation? Could the soacked satchel have been hauled out of the river just before the water seeped onto the cover of the book? Who knows?

Back in the library, the monks took writing books very seriously. They created incredibly colourful pages, using ink that they kept in little horns. If a mistake was made in a book, the monks could get very upset. Columba, on the other hand, didn't lose his cool over this sort of thing.

Once, a monk came up to Columba and asked if the book he had just finished could be checked for any mistakes. According to one report Columba replied, 'There's no need to check it. Everything is fine except, in one place, the letter 'I' is missing. It's no big deal.'

But how could Columba know that without even looking at a single page of the book? When the monk looked

through the book himself, he was astonished. Apparently, there was an 'I' missing just as Columba had said. If this report is true, it seems that his special powers never ceased to amaze his brother monks, just as magicians today never cease to amaze people with their ability to read cards without even looking at them. On the other hand, there could be a perfectly rational explanation. Perhaps Columba had been secretly checking up on the monk's work whenever he went for a break? You decide.

After a while, despite the odd spelling mistake, Columba and his monks filled the library with many useful books. We don't know exactly what was in the library, but there might have been some books that were similar to these titles!

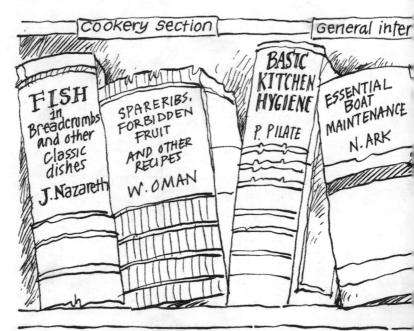

Near the library and other huts was a cemetery, where dead monks were buried. This might seem like a sad place, but it was built close by so that old friends would not be forgotten. What's more, the Columbans believed that when you died it wasn't the end of you – but only the beginning. Your soul went to Heaven where you lived happily ever after. In fact, another of Columba's special powers was that he could apparently see good people's souls being carried by angels to Heaven after they died.

Mind you, there was always a danger that the body of a nice old monk might get dug up and gobbled by a hungry wolf or other wild animal. So a wall was built to protect the monastery from any uninvited guests.

But sometimes even the wall wasn't enough to keep out the fiercest of wild animals. While other monks ran and hid in cupboards or frantically tried to climb onto the roof, it was left to Columba to use his special powers to save the day. With a wave of Columba's hand, we are told that wolves and other scary beasts that got into the monastery were either tamed or driven away.

This sounds like another miracle. On the other hand, it could be that Columba used skills that any normal person can learn. Expert animal trainers, for example, have the power to make all kinds of creatures do exactly what they command.

One thing's for sure, if an ordinary person without such special talents tried such heroics they would be eaten alive – but not Columba. Soon the word spread around the neighbouring islands that Columba of Iona was a man with extraordinary powers. Before long, people began turning up at his door begging for help . . .

9

Good news, bad news

A new hut was built at the monastery just for guests, where they could wait for an appointment with Columba. It was a bit like waiting to see the doctor at a hospital, or an officer at the police station. Except Columba was no mere doctor or policeman. He was a miracle-worker.

Columba's visitors were dazzled when he seemed to turn water into wine.

They were overjoyed when Columba seemed to cure their sick relatives.

And they were astounded when he convinced them he could see into the future.

But when people came to Columba looking for help, they didn't always get the answers they were looking for.

The strong man went away and eventually forgot about Columba's prediction. One day, he was sitting under an upturned boat, stripping bark from a long stick with his knife. Suddenly he heard a row break out among some men nearby and got up to stop the fight. But during this quick movement, he wounded his knee very badly with his own knife. Too late, the strong man realised what Columba meant – his killer was his trusty knife! Sure enough, the wound on his knee never healed and a few months later the strong man died.

If it is true that Columba predicted this, then maybe he would have been better off keeping it to himself! But just because he sometimes foretold people's deaths, doesn't mean Columba was cruel or heartless. Perhaps he was just trying to give people an honest answer – without hurting their feelings too much if the answer wasn't what they wanted to hear.

Columba didn't just work miracles – he also cared about justice, law and order. So he was a bit like a policeman. Once he was told about a greedy thief who was stealing seal pups from a nearby island. Columba instructed two trusted monks to go out and find the thief, who was discovered hiding under an upturned boat.

The monks told the thief that he would be given whatever food and drink he needed to live a comfortable life, provided he agreed to stop stealing. Fearing what Columba might do to him if he disobeyed, the thief agreed to change his ways.

Columba relied on his monks to do a lot of important work for him, because he couldn't be everywhere at once. So it was very important that new monks were recruited to join the monastery. Luckily, there seems to have been no shortage of willing volunteers. Young island men knew that if they joined the monastery they would not only learn about religion, they would learn all sorts of really important stuff.

HAVE YOU EVER CONSIDERED A CAREER AS A MONK? APPLY NOW!!

FULL TRAINING GIVEN IN...

* Religious Studies   * Gardening
* Shoe & clothes making * Cookery
* Fishing & farming   * Woodwork
* Sailing & rowing   * Metalwork
* Leatherwork   * Book making

FREE FERRY SERVICE TO IONA PROVIDED

As the months and years went by, students came to Iona from far and wide.

Eventually, Columba's community grew so big and busy that he decided he needed a change of scene – a chance to get away from it all. So he decided to go on a holiday, exploring more islands . . .

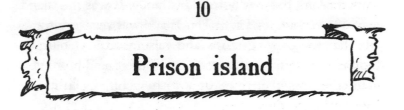

10

Prison island

Columba was one of Scotland's first tourists. But instead of shorts and a towel in his rucksack he had religious stuff like his Bible and his prayer rope – which was a simple necklace with lots of knots in it that

I fancy a change of scene. Anyone coming?

reminded him how many prayers he'd said.

Because the islands of the Hebrides were all quite close together, Columba was able to hop from island to island. Okay, he didn't hop, he took a boat – but you get the idea.

Some islands were still difficult and even dangerous to get to – especially when there was a storm. There is a report of one occasion when Columba sailed through a storm that was so bad the waves rose up as high as mountains. Apparently, Columba had to use his special powers to calm the water and allow his boat to reach its destination safely. At least that's what the people on the boat believed.

After sailing about for a while, Columba came across another island that really took his fancy. It was the island known to us today as Tiree. This island was very fertile and excellent for growing crops and raising cattle. Columba decided to set up another monastery there and brought a team of monks over from Iona to help him build it. He called it Mag Luinge.

But Columba didn't stop there. He discovered another island, called Hinba, and decided to set up a third monastery there.

When the new monastery on Hinba was ready, Columba used it to host some very special visitors. These visitors included other important churchmen who had heard about all the good work Columba was doing and wanted to meet him.

But Hinba also hosted some less agreeable visitors. Apparently this was the place where Columba decided to put people who had done really bad things – terrible crimes like beating somebody up or killing them. So Hinba was also a prison island.

One of the prisoners in Hinba jail was an outlaw known as Lam Dess, which means 'Right Hand'. Maybe he lost his left hand in a battle – who knows.

Lam Dess was a really nasty piece of work – and he wanted revenge on Columba for locking him up. One day, when Columba was going about his business on Hinba, Lam Dess broke free and tried to kill him. But Columba was too fast and managed to duck out of the way.

That was the last mistake Lam Dess ever made. Not long afterwards, when Columba was paying a visit to Iona, he turned on his powers of 'second sight'. In those days, people believed that second sight allowed a person to see things that were happening many miles away. On this occasion, Columba claimed he could see Lam Dess being killed in a brawl – probably for stepping out of line once too often.

Even though Hinba was a very important island, amazingly nobody today knows for sure exactly where it was. It has become a mystery island.

That doesn't mean Hinba has disappeared or sunk into the sea. It just means that the island goes by a different name these days and nobody can remember which one it is.

It is said that Hinba had a very long narrow sea loch, which cut deep into the island. This means Hinba could be the island of Jura, which is near Iona and does have a long sea loch. Jura also has a small, very old church on it called a chapel. This might be the site where Columba built his Hinba monastery.

It's a shame we don't know for sure where Hinba was, because it was here that one of the key events in Columba's story happened.

IT'S SAID THAT COLUMBA BELIEVED HE WAS VISITED BY AN ANGEL WHO HANDED HIM A GLASS BOOK. THE BOOK CONTAINED A MESSAGE FROM GOD.

Seek out a man called Aedan and crown him king of DAL RIATA

59

Columba apparently thought about this. He really didn't fancy getting lashed yet again. But more importantly, he thought that perhaps Aedan deserved a chance to prove himself. Plus agreeing to this task might have been another way for Columba to make up for his bad deeds at the Battle of Cul Drebene, all those years ago. It could have been another way of completing his penance.

But who exactly was Aedan, anyway? Where was Dal Riata? And how come Columba had the job of crowning its king?

11

The sea kingdom

Columba didn't have to look for long before he found Aedan. It seems that when our hero paid a return visit to Iona in the year 574, Aedan and his entourage were there at the monastery waiting for him.

Aedan explained that the old king, who was called Conall, had died. As Conall's cousin, it was now Aedan's turn to become king.

I ask you to give me a blessing. This would make me a more respected king since you, Columba, are such a special and popular man.

Columba was happy to oblige. He sat Aedan down on a coronation stone, which might even have been the stone pillow Columba slept on at night! And why not? Stones can have many uses.

Many people believe Columba's stone was the Stone of Destiny, which was used for centuries afterwards to crown Scottish kings. It can be seen today in Edinburgh Castle.

Columba put a mark on Aedan's forehead with a sweet-smelling holy oil called 'chrism'. This was called 'anointing'. It was believed to be a stamp of approval from God.

Apparently, this was the first time in the history of Britain that a Christian churchman had given a new king his blessing. So it was a very special occasion.

62

We can imagine there must have been a great celebration afterwards. Columba and Aedan quickly became friends. In fact, Columba predicted that Aedan would be victorious in battle. He also told Aedan that as long as his family were good they would always be kings. Apparently, in later years, Aedan was indeed victorious in battle as Columba predicted. Just a coincidence? Or proof that Columba really could read the future? You decide.

In return, Aedan told Columba about his kingdom – Dal Riata. Of course, this was not the first time that Columba had heard of Dal Riata. In fact, the late King Conall had probably given Columba permission to build his monasteries on Iona, Hinba and Tiree.

But now, thanks to his new friend King Aedan, Columba learned more details. Here are some facts about Dal Riata. Some of these Columba probably knew already, some he might have learned from Aedan – and a few are details that only we know:

FACTS about DAL RIATA

- AREA: KNOWN TODAY AS ARGYLL
- PROBABLY CREATED AROUND 500 A.D.
- MAIN LANGUAGE: GAELIC (SIMILAR TO IRISH GAELIC WHICH COLUMBA SPOKE. SOME PEOPLE KNEW LATIN, TOO.)
- THE PEOPLE WERE KNOWN AS SCOTS OR SCOTII.
- FIRST KING CAME FROM ANTRIM IN THE NORTH OF IRELAND (THOUGH SOME HISTORIANS THINK THE SCOTS HAD ALWAYS BEEN IN DAL RIATA).
- MAIN MEANS OF TRAVEL: BOAT.
- TRADE: TRADERS BROUGHT WINE, FABRICS, DYES FOR CLOTHES, JEWELLERY AND WEAPONS (FROM AS FAR AWAY AS FRANCE AND ROME) IN RETURN FOR FUR, LEATHER GOODS AND SLAVES.
- OTHER FACTS: THE PEOPLE OF DAL RIATA WERE ADVANCED BY DARK AGE STANDARDS. THEY KEPT WRITTEN RECORDS ABOUT THE INHABITANTS AND THE TAX THEY PAID. OTHER INFORMATION WAS MEMORISED BY BARDS WHO KEPT THE HISTORY OF THE PEOPLE IN THEIR HEADS.

The capital of Dal Riata was a place called Dunadd, which people can still visit today. There is a large flat stone in the ground at Dal Riata with a footprint carved in the rock. When he became king, Aedan had to put his foot in the rock. This was a signal that he was married to the land. The idea was that the land would give good harvests for Aedan's people.

Aedan's people were, of course, the Scots. The kingdom was like a big extended family, with Aedan at its head. The family had many branches, called Cenel. As you have discovered, this means 'children'. It also means 'clan'. This was how the Scottish clans we know today began.

Aedan told all the clans that, from now on, Columba was Dal Riata's religious leader. The king made Iona the most holy place in the kingdom – and decreed that all future kings had to be anointed and buried there. This made Dal Riata a Christian kingdom. If we remember that Columba might have been on a mission to make up for past mistakes, then becoming Dal Riata's religious leader was a big step in the right direction. But there was still more work to be done.

The Scots of Dal Riata were surrounded by other king-doms. The people of these neighbouring kingdoms had many confusing names and languages.

Now, in a way, all the kingdoms of Scotland were Scottish – it's just that they didn't go by that name in those days, because they hadn't decided to join together as one kingdom yet. But they all lived on the land that we know today as Scotland. And they had dealings with each other that would eventually bring them closer and closer together in unity. Except, in Columba's day, they mostly couldn't stand each other.

Confused? Well, it gets worse. All these different kingdoms spoke in different tongues. As we have already learned, the Scots of Dal Riata spoke Gaelic. But the Britons spoke a language that was similar to Welsh. As for the Angles, they spoke a language that sounded a bit like English. Only English then sounded a bit like the Scots language sounds today, which is not to be confused with Gaelic . . .

But we are forgetting some people. Wild, scary, painted people known as Picts. Now it was Aedan's turn to learn a few things from Columba – because Columba had already been to visit the Picts. It was quite an adventure . . .

12

Painted people

About two years after he first arrived in Scotland, Columba decided to visit a mountain kingdom to the north and east of Dal Riata. It was called Pictland – home of the Picts. Before he set out, Columba's library on Iona might have told him a few things about the Picts . . .

In Columba's day the Romans were long gone and hadn't written down much about the Picts. So the Picts were very mysterious. But Columba wanted to find out more. According to reports, the Picts were not Christians and had never heard of God. So Columba planned to convert them! This was his mission – and that's why he is often called a 'missionary'. If he was successful, God would surely be pleased with him.

Gathering together a fellowship of trusty companions, Columba headed off in search of the Picts' mysterious mountain kingdom . . .

After journeying for a while, by boat and on foot, Columba came across some strange, upright stones. These stones were carved with curious symbols like fish, horses, bulls and other animals. They also showed everyday items like combs and mirrors.

But what did the symbols mean? Perhaps they were Dark Age advertisements, a bit like the posters we see on bus shelters today? So if Columba wanted to buy a mirror or a horse, maybe he had come to the right place.

Although there were standing stones in Dal Riata, the stones Columba stumbled across now were different from anything he had seen before. He realised he must have crossed the border into Pictland . . .

13

Dark water

As Columba continued his travels, he came to the banks of a river that we know today as the River Ness. There he met some Pictish people. These Picts spoke a very old-fashioned language that the Columbans could vaguely understand – it sounded like a mix of tongues, including Scottish Gaelic and Latin.

Not that the Picts were in much of a mood for conversation. They were burying one of their friends. The Picts told Columba that their friend had been swimming in the river when he was suddenly mauled by a huge water beast – a monster.

His friends had rushed out onto the water in a little boat to rescue him, but they were too late. All they could do was reach out with their fishing hooks and pull in his poor, dead body.

When Columba heard this story, we are told that he did an astonishing thing. He instructed one of his companions, a young lad called Luigne Moccu Min, to swim across the river and sail back in a little boat that was on the opposite bank. Without hesitation, Luigne obeyed his master. He dived into the river and began swimming. The Picts thought he must be mad.

So can you guess what happened next? If you remember from the start of our story, the water beast was lying on the riverbed. It was still hungry. Its first victim had only whetted its appetite – and now it wanted more!

Just as it was about to have its second course, the creature was jerked back by Columba's special powers – or so it seemed to the people who were watching. Whatever the cause, the monster swam away and disappeared.

Luigne made it safely to the other side and eventually returned in the little boat. As he thanked Columba for saving his life, Columba's friends explained to the awe-struck Picts what they had just witnessed. It's a kind of magic, they said, but it's much more powerful. It's a miracle – the work of God! That's what they believed, anyway.

Of course, the monster might not have been quite as big as the reports suggest. Perhaps it was a bearded seal – or a walrus. But on the other hand, it might have been a huge prehistoric creature that we know today as . . . Nessie!

The taming of Nessie – or whatever it was – got the Picts thinking. Up until then, very few of them had ever heard of 'miracles' or 'God'. Most of them knew nothing about the Christian Church.

Instead they believed in magic and had not one God, but many gods. They worshipped the sun, the moon and the stars. They also worshipped trees, streams, plants and lakes. In other words, they worshipped nature. The Christian word for someone who worships nature is a 'pagan'.

Pagan priests are sometimes referred to as druids. They were wizards, or sorcerers, and they practised magic.

So what sort of magic did the pagan Picts believe in? Columba soon found out when he went to visit a village well.

It is said that from then on the well was transformed. Instead of causing disease, people believed that its water cured their illnesses.

News of Columba's healing hands, wisdom and fearlessness spread like wildfire around Pictland. Apparently, people began queuing up to throw off their old pagan ways and become Christians. But Columba realised that in order to make sure the Picts changed their ways for good, he would have to go right to the top.

14

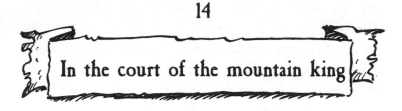

In the court of the mountain king

The ruler of Pictland was King Bridei. He was not an easy man to reach and, according to some reports, he was a nasty piece of work. The path to his castle was long and steep. It sat on a hilltop looking over the Beauly Firth. The hilltop is known today as Craig Phadraig.

Eventually, after a long and tiring walk, Columba and his companions reached the castle walls. So did they get a warm welcome? Fat chance.

The king ordered his castle guards not to let the Christians in. Bridei was a proud king who had ruled for more than ten years. He wasn't too pleased about this newcomer Columba, who was going around dazzling his subjects with miracles.

But, as you have discovered, Columba was a very persistent chap. He had a mission and was determined to accomplish it. Plus he had his penance to think about. Making sure all the Picts converted to Christianity might have been the last hurdle Columba had to jump over to please God – and make up for his war crime.

So instead of turning around and going away, Columba walked right up to the castle doors. He made a sign of the cross. Then he reached out with his hand and gave the doors a knock.

In an instant, the bars that locked the doors from the inside could be heard sliding away. Then the doors threw themselves open. To Columba's companions, it looked like their leader's powers had done the trick yet again. But maybe somebody on the inside had changed their mind and decided to open the door by hand. Who knows?

Anyway, Columba walked in, followed by his friends. King Bridei couldn't believe it – to him, it looked like Columba had used some kind of magic to open the doors.

King Bridei couldn't believe it – he had given strict orders the the doors be kept shut! He waited for Columba to do something really terrible to him with his magic. But, of course, Columba's power was not magic – it was the power of God. Columba told Bridei that he had nothing to fear, as long as he gave up his pagan ways and agreed to become a Christian.

Bridei realised that Columba meant business and started treating him with more respect. But the king still wasn't convinced that Columba was anything more than an especially powerful pagan wizard. So he suggested a contest, to see if Columba's god really was stronger than the gods of nature worshipped by pagans.

Bridei pitched Columba and his so-called miracles against the pagan powers of the royal magician, who was called Broichan.

So what was the competition?

1. To see which one could pull the most rabbits out of a hat in a minute?
2. To see who could saw their glamorous assistant in half without hurting them?
3. To see which one could make a body float in the air with no strings attached?

Well, Briochan and Columba probably performed all kinds of dazzling tricks, just as a magician might today. But after a while Columba grew tired of the competition and got down to more serious business . . .

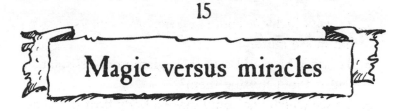

15

Magic versus miracles

Columba decided to lay down a challenge of his own. He turned to Briochan and said something along these lines.

Columba and his friends left the castle, leaving Briochan and Bridei to think he had given up and gone home. But instead, Columba was on his way back to the River Ness. On the banks, he picked up a stone and told his companions that the stone was blessed by God – and could now heal sick people. The monks looked at each other, not quite sure what Columba was up to.

Sure enough, so the story goes, back at the castle an angel from Heaven had appeared. We are told that the angel hit Briochan with a bolt of energy, shattering a glass cup in Briochan's hands into fragments. Then it gripped Briochan's neck with some invisible force so he couldn't breathe. His face turned blue.

Now, maybe Briochan wasn't *really* gripped by a godly power – but it is certainly possible that he believed he was. And that could have been enough to make him think he was about to croak.

Either way, Briochan seemed to be close to death, so King Bridei sent two messengers to fetch Columba for help. When the messengers appeared at the river, Columba gave the blessed stone to two of his companions and said.

Make sure Briochan promises to release the girl first. Then, and only then, dip this stone in some water and let him drink it. He will be well again immediately. If he refuses to let her go, don't give him any blessed water – he will die on the spot.

The two Columbans followed the king's men back to the castle. When they told the king everything Columba had said, Bridei was terrified. Bridei persuaded Briochan to agree to Columba's demand. So the slave girl was set free and handed over to Columba's messengers.

But what happened to Briochan? Just as Columba had asked, his men put the stone in some water. Instead of sinking, as stones should, we are told that this stone floated on the surface of the water like an apple or a nut. Everyone was amazed – even though Columba might have tricked them by giving his men a piece of wood that looked like a stone instead of the real thing.

Briochan was given some of the water to drink and he quickly began to feel better. Perhaps it really was a miracle. Or maybe Briochan just believed so strongly that it would cure him that his mind made him better? Either way, everyone was amazed again.

After that, King Bridei was very impressed with Columba. But what about Briochan? Did he accept defeat and congratulate Columba? No chance.

He has belittled me and humiliated me! I shall get my own back!

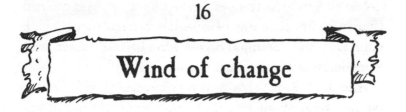

16

Wind of change

One day, when Columba was preparing to leave Pictland and sail down Loch Ness back to Dal Riata, we are told that Briochan approached him.

But Briochan wasn't put off his nasty plan. When Columba arrived at the head of Loch Ness, a great crowd of people gathered to see if Briochan's magic would block Columba's way. Soon, according to reports, a great mist covered the loch and a stormy wind began blowing against Columba.

But Columba stayed cool, calm and collected. He boarded his boat and ordered his men to hoist the sail. Even though the wind was now blowing against the boat with fury, the boat sailed forward at great speed. The crowd on the shore were gobsmacked – even though Columba might have cunningly told one of his monks to use a hidden oar to push the boat along without anybody seeing.

After a few moments the wind apparently turned around and became a gentle breeze that blew in the boat's favour, pushing it along the loch with ease. As the boat carried on down the loch, reports from the scene suggest that many Picts watching from the shore decided that miracles really were more powerful than magic. Briochan and the other pagan wizards were beaten once and for all.

After that, Columba probably made many return visits to Pictland. And King Bridei was happy to welcome him. With Bridei on his side, each time Columba returned he was able to persuade more and more Picts to join his Church.

On his travels, Columba went even further than Pictland. He probably journeyed south to the kingdom of the Britons of Strathclyde. There, he made friends with the ruler, King Roderc.

It is possible that Columba visited King Roderc at his castle on Dumbarton Rock. Apparently the two men got on like a house on fire.

On Columba's return visits to Dal Riata, King Aedan must have been very impressed when he heard about our hero's successful battles against pagan wizards in Pictland and his travels among the Britons.

So had Columba finally done enough to end his penance and make up for his war crime at the Battle of Cul Drebene all those years ago? Could he now put his feet up and relax, safe in the knowledge that he would be welcomed into the kingdom of Heaven when he died? These were important questions, since Columba wasn't a young man any more. By now, he might have been growing quite old.

To find out the answers, he decided to do something he had vowed he would never do. He was going to journey to a place where a lot of people might be out to get him for his part in the Battle of Cul Drebene. It was an extremely dangerous place.

That's right, Columba was going back to where he came from . . .

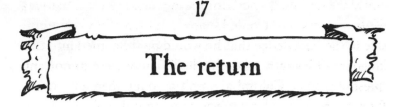

17

The return

Columba set sail for Ireland. Along the way he stopped for a bit at an island halfway between there and Scotland. It was called Rathlin Island.

While Columba was on Rathlin, perhaps sheltering from a storm or stocking up on food, a man came up to him looking very upset.

Columba asked what the matter was. The poor fellow said that his wife didn't like him because she thought he was too ugly! Luckily, Columba managed to persuade the man's wife to see that personality is more important than looks – and that seemed to do the trick.

I must remember to have marriage guidance councillor added to my business card.

No doubt feeling a warm glow, Columba set sail from Rathlin towards Ireland. But hang on a minute. Hadn't Columba been banished from Ireland and excommunicated? Well, it turns out that news of all his good work in Scotland had found its way back to Ireland, what with all the ships to-ing and fro-ing. By this time he was probably back in the Church's good books in Ireland – even though there were probably some Irish people who still had it in for him because of his old battling days.

But what about Columba himself? Hadn't he vowed that he would never, ever return to Ireland?

According to reports, not only had Columba promised he would never set foot on Irish soil again, he had also promised not to look at any Irish men, women, girls or boys or eat any Irish food or drink. So how on Earth was he going to visit the place?

Apparently, he had a cunning plan. In his boat, Columba had a large piece of Scottish turf – which was a chunk of earth covered in grass. When his boat arrived in Ireland, we are told that the Scottish turf was rolled out in front of him on the shore by his companions.

So when Columba stepped off the boat, his feet were not actually *on* Irish soil. Very clever.

So much for not stepping on Irish soil. But he could still see Ireland, couldn't he? No, he couldn't. We are told that he brought a blindfold with him. His friends kept him blindfolded at all times so he couldn't see anyone, or anything. Very, very clever.

But what about Irish food and drink? Surely he needed to eat something while he was there? Not at all. Columba, apparently, had thought his plan through. His boat was loaded with food and water from Scotland, so there was no need to touch any Irish stuff during his visit.

The trouble with being blindfolded, on the other hand, is that you face all sorts of hidden hazards. And it wasn't long before Columba ran into danger.

In order to travel around Ireland without putting his foot on Irish soil Columba needed transport. So his companions found a chariot.

Before stepping on board, Columba gave the chariot his blessing with a sign of the cross. It's just as well he did, because the chariot seems to have had a dangerous flaw. For some strange reason, so the story goes, the linchpins holding the wheels in place were missing. This meant the wheels could come flying off at high speed, causing the chariot to crash!

Perhaps the linchpins had been removed deliberately by someone who was still angry at Columba over the Battle of Cul Drebene? Who knows?

The chariot was driven by a man called Colman, who set off at great speed to take Columba to a monastery far away. As the chariot shook and bounced along the rocky and boggy Irish roads, Colman had no idea what peril he and Columba were in.

Amazingly, after a long day on the road, the chariot arrived safely at its destination. When Colman happened to look at the wheels he was horrified to see the linchpins were missing – yet relieved they hadn't crashed.

Columba's special powers had saved the day again – or

so it would seem. He was able to go about his business in Ireland without any more trouble.

This was a good sign. Maybe God was satisfied with Columba at last? Maybe he had finally done his penance? If so, it was just as well, because Columba could not live forever.

After a while in Ireland, he returned to his monastery on Iona and carried on his work – while he prepared for his most important journey ever . . .

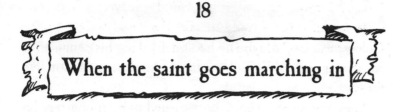

18

When the saint goes marching in

It's said that, in May 597, Columba realised he had only a short time to live. He was now about seventy-six – very old for a Dark Age person. So he set about taking care of last minute business.

One day, while he was giving a blessing to a cart of grain, he turned to one of his helpers and said . . .

When the midnight bell sounded that night, despite being very weak, Columba got up and rushed as fast as he could to the church.

At the altar, he dropped to his knees to pray. The other monks poured into the church behind him.

It's said a halo of bright light seemed to appear around Columba. Suddenly, the light faded – leaving the monks groping about for the old man in the dark.

Diormit, one of Columba's closest friends, found him. As Diormit rested Columba's head on his lap, other monks reappeared carrying lamps.

At that moment, Columba passed away – and the monks believed they saw him breathe out his soul with his last breath. It was a few minutes past midnight. A new day, Sunday 9 June, had just begun.

As far as Christians then and now are concerned, Columba's soul rose up to Heaven – where he began a new life. Not only that, he was about to become a saint – a very special member of the Church. He was now . . . Saint Columba. And God had forgiven his sins!

Once in Heaven, Columba might have bumped into a few other Scottish saints who turned up there over the centuries . . .

Nice to meet you, Columba! My name's Saint Andrew – Scotland's patron saint. It's funny, though – I've never been to the place! I'm from Galilee myself. Still, it's nice that I'm an inspiration to the Scottish people – just as you are – that's what really matters, eh?

Back down on Iona, Columba's funeral had lasted for three days. It's said the weather was stormy and nobody could reach the island. So the only guests were Columba's closest brother monks – who believed they could see angels and Heavenly lights at his graveside.

The monks put Columba's stone pillow next to his grave as a monument. Nobody knows for sure where Columba's grave is today, but some people believe you can still find it on Iona.

The moment Columba was buried, reports say, the weather became calm.

See! The old man's controlling life on Iona from beyond the grave!

So what did the monks from Iona and Columba's other monasteries do next? Did they forget about being monks and decide to do something else instead?

Of course not. They carried on Columba's work, which is still going strong today . . .

Saint Columba is a hero anyone can admire. It doesn't matter whether you are religious or not. And it doesn't matter whether you think stories about miracles are true or not. In fact, you don't have to believe in God to be inspired by Columba's amazing life.

The Columba we have learned about believed he could make the world a better place. He was brave. He was adventurous. He was tough but fair. He was a hard worker. He learned from his mistakes – and he was loyal to his friends.

The stories about Columba's miracles and visions might not be quite how things really happened, but – as we said at the beginning – that depends on whether or not you believe in miracles. It's up to you. One thing's for sure, Columba was a remarkable person.

Inspired by Columba's example, his monks travelled back to Pictland to finish off what he had started. Thanks to Columba, and other Scottish saints, eventually the whole of Scotland became Christian.

Why is that a good thing? Well, thanks to people studying the Bible, many things improved over the years – especially basic stuff like reading and writing.

Meanwhile, more books were added to Columba's library at Iona, which grew into an even more powerful and important place. These books included the *Book of Kells*, which is now kept in Ireland. The *Book of Kells* is a copy of the gospels of the Bible and its pages are beautifully illustrated.

All the while, stories, songs and poems about Columba's life were told and retold. Some of them were myths, but others contained solid facts about Columba's real life.

Speaking of hard evidence, did you know that there are Columban artefacts you can still look at today? One of the most famous is in the National Museum in Edinburgh. It's a little metal box called the Brecbennach, or Monymusk Reliquary. It is said to contain tiny bits of Columba's bones – which are believed to bring the Scots good luck in battle.

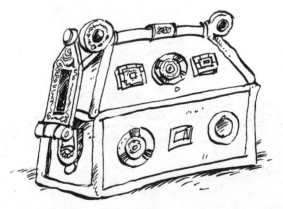

And there's the Stone of Destiny – the stone pillow on which Columba anointed Aedan king. It was moved from Columba's grave and is now kept in Edinburgh Castle. But some people say it's a fake. Why not take a look and decide for yourself?

There are, of course, other ways to get up close to Columba. One day you might visit Gartan in County Donegal, Ireland, to look for his birthplace.

Nobody knows for sure where exactly Columba was born. But if you can find a stone with a cross-shaped groove in it, you might be standing on the very spot.

The best way to make a connection with Columba is to visit the Scottish island that he made his home – Iona. Today, the church that Columba set up there is still flourishing.

The original wooden huts are long gone, but the place still echoes with memories of long ago. There's even a road there called the 'Street of the Dead'.

If you ever get a chance to visit Iona, keep your eyes peeled. You never know if the spirit of Saint Columba might be waiting there to greet you.